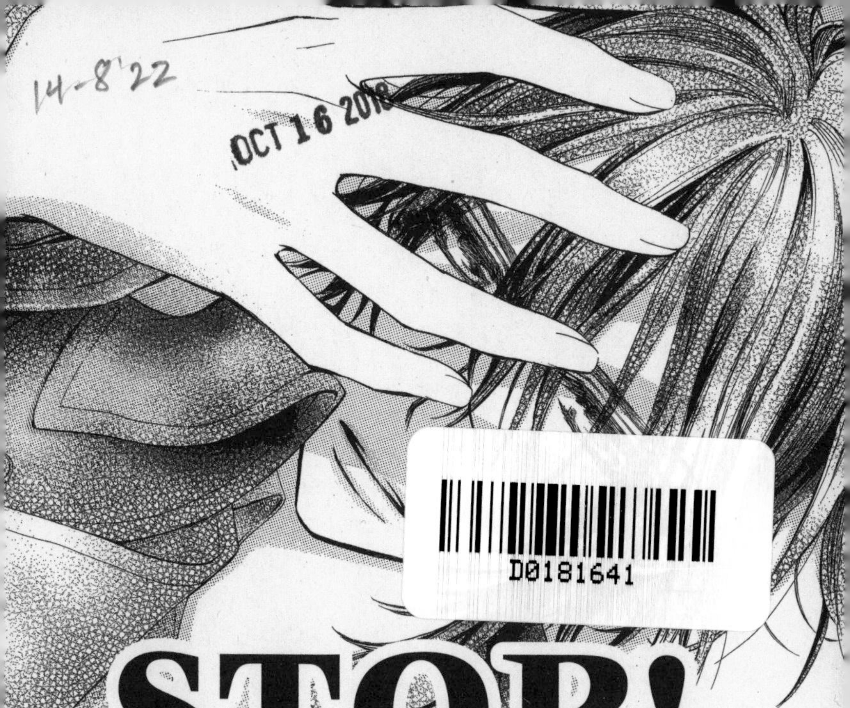

STOP!

You may be reading the wrong way!

In keeping with the original Japanese comic format, this book reads from right to left—so word balloons, action and sound effects and are reversed to preserve the orientation of the original artwork.

Check out the diagram shown here to get the hang of things, and then turn to the other side of the book to get started!

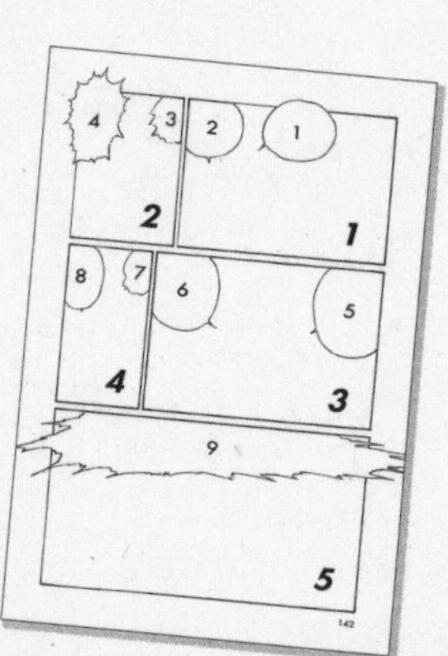

Shojo Beat

VAMPIRE KNIGHT MEMORIES

VOLUME

2

STORY & ART BY

Matsuri Hino

The Story of VAMPIRE KNIGHT

Previously...

Vampire Knight is the story of Yuki Kuran, a pureblood vampire princess who was brought up as a human.
A moment of peace has arrived after a fierce battle between humans and vampires. But Kaname Kuran, whose heart has become the Ancestor Metal for weapons capable of killing vampires, continues to sleep within a coffin of ice. A thousand years later, Yuki gives Kaname her heart, and he is revived as a human. Yuki and Kaname's daughter, Ai, begins to tell him about the days that have passed...
Yuki's friend Sayori Wakaba stays close to Hanabusa Aido while he searches for a way to turn vampires into humans, yet Sayori has chosen to remain human. Meanwhile, Zero Kiryu continues to support the bereaved Yuki. They love each other but are unable to move forward due to their roles. But after enough time passes, they finally take a step forward...

CHARACTERS

YUKI KURAN (CROSS)

The adopted daughter of the headmaster of Cross Academy. She is a pureblood vampire and the princess of the noble Kuran family. She has always adored Kaname, even when she did not have her memory.

KANAME KURAN

A pureblood vampire and the progenitor of the Kurans. He is Yuki's fiancé and was raised as her sibling. He knows Yuki's true identity and cares for her...

ZERO KIRYU

He was born into a family of vampire hunters and later was turned into a vampire. His parents were killed by a pureblood. He has agonized over his feelings for Yuki and his role as a vampire hunter.

REN AND AI

Yuki's children

HANABUSA AIDO

He was an upperclassman in the Night Class. He is working to create a medicine that will turn vampires into humans...

CONTENTS

VAMPIRE KNIGHT MEMORIES

THE WARMTH OF THE PRINCESS OF MY MEMORIES

YOU MUST HAVE PRACTICED A LOT. GOOD WORK.

ALL FOR TODAY...

I TOLD YOU I'M ONLY NOW REVEALING MY TRUE POWERS!

YOU TWO ARE SLEEPY...? VAMPIRES ARE NOCTURNAL, AREN'T THEY?
YAWN
I'M SLEEPY... I CAN'T STAY UP ANYMORE. I HAVEN'T SLEPT IN AGES...

BOTH OF YOU...
...COME FROM THE PERSON I LOVED.
I KNOW FROM OBSERVING YOU...
...THAT SHE TOO CHERISHED HER TIME WITH YOU.
AND THERE'S SOME-THING MORE...
MY ONLY REMAINING MEMORY IS FROM A TIME I CANNOT RECALL.
IT'S OF A GIRL WHO SUDDENLY APPEARED BEFORE ME LIKE A MIRAGE ON A BATTLE-FIELD...

I HAD ALWAYS WANTED TO MEET HER AGAIN.
I HAD THE FEELING I WOULD.
THE TWO BEFORE ME ARE THE LAST VESTIGES OF YOU...
AND YOU YOURSELF ARE RIGHT HERE...

IT'S AS IF YOU'RE TELLING ME THAT I NEEDN'T REMEMBER...
...MY DAYS WITH YOU.

YUKI...

BECAUSE I'M RIGHT HERE.

SHE SAID THAT TO ME.

HEH HEH HEH.

JEALOUS, AREN'T YOU?

I'M THE ONE WHO GETS TO HUG HER LIKE THIS ALL THE TIME.

—1—

Vampire Knight Memories Volume 2

Thank you very much for picking up this volume.

Memories is a series I am working on gratefully as a way to supplement the final chapter of *Vampire Knight* volume 19.

When I started working on the fourth chapter, the decision was made for this to become an ongoing series.

This is all thanks to the support of my readers.

Thank you very much.

(continues ↓)

MAYBE I SHOULD MAKE AI START WRITING ABOUT HERSELF MORE.
BACK THEN, I HAD NO IDEA THAT...
...SEVERAL DECADES LATER...
...I WOULD START WITH YUKI AGAIN FROM SCRATCH...
...AND END UP ANNOUNCING OUR RELATIONSHIP TO EVERYONE.
I'M SURE AI HAS SECRETS SHE DOESN'T WANT ME TO KNOW...
THERE WERE TOO MANY WHO WERE UNABLE TO IGNORE OUR RELATIONSHIP DUE TO VARIOUS REASONS.
FOR EXAMPLE...

...SAYORI WAKABA HERE.
SHE SEEMS ANGRY.
I HAVEN'T SEEN YOU FOR AGES, ZERO. ARE YOU ATTENDING A LECTURE TODAY?
YEAH.
I NEED TO FIND OUT HOW MUCH RESEARCH THE UNIVERSITY HAS ON VAMPIRES FOR THE HUNTER SOCIETY.
AND I'VE GOT MY MAIN JOB TOO, SO IT'S TAKING ME FOREVER TO GET THE CREDITS I NEED...
WHAT ABOUT YOU, WAKABA?
I'M HELPING MY FATHER OUT. I CAME HERE TO ASK A PROFESSOR IF HE COULD PROVIDE DOCUMENTS TO USE IN CONGRESS.
AND I'M GETTING THE CAKES THAT HANABUSA LOVES ON THE WAY BACK.
HMM...
SHE SEEMS GLOOMY.
WHAT IS IT?
HOW ARE THINGS?

HOW ARE YOU AND YUKI DOING?
HUH?
ARE YOU GETTING MARRIED OR NOT?
WHAT?
IF YOU ARE, WOULD YOU PLEASE HURRY UP?
UH...?
HANABUSA IS ASKING...
"AM I EVEN ALLOWED TO GET MARRIED BEFORE THE PUREBLOOD WHOM I SERVE?!"
HE'S BEING SUCH A LOYAL DOG THAT WE'RE NOT GETTING ANYWHERE BECAUSE OF IT.
IS HE STUPID?
WHAT A PAIN.
SORRY. THIS ISN'T YOUR PROBLEM.
I'M FEELING A BIT PRESSED BECAUSE I'LL END UP BECOMING AN OLD MAID AT THIS RATE...
I SHOULDN'T HAVE SAID ANYTHING.

...
PLEASE FORGET WHAT I JUST SAID.
HAVE YOU... THOUGHT ABOUT ASKING YUKI?
WHAT?
MMBL
TO GRANT YOU THE LONGEVITY OF A VAMPIRE.
HANABUSA OFFERED ME THE SAME THING ONCE...
I SEE.
OKAY, I'M GOING THIS WAY.
ENJOY THE LECTURE.
YEAH.

EVEN THOUGH I DID ASK YOU TO FORGET WHAT I SAID...
...I'VE ALWAYS SUPPORTED YOUR RELATIONSHIP. THAT WON'T CHANGE.
THANKS.
OOH, LOOK! IT'S SHADY!
IT'S BEEN A WHILE SINCE I SAW YOU ATTEND A LECTURE.
WHY DO YOU CALL HIM "SHADY"?
BECAUSE HE'S ALWAYS IN THE SHADE.
AH! RIGHT...
DON'T YOU THINK IT'S ABOUT TIME YOU TOLD ME YOUR NAME?
HEY! DON'T YOU LIKE PEOPLE WHO ARE FRIENDLY?

AH!
HEY.
DON'T IGNORE ME.

I HOPE SUP-PORTING THEIR RELATION-SHIP...
...IS THE RIGHT THING TO DO.

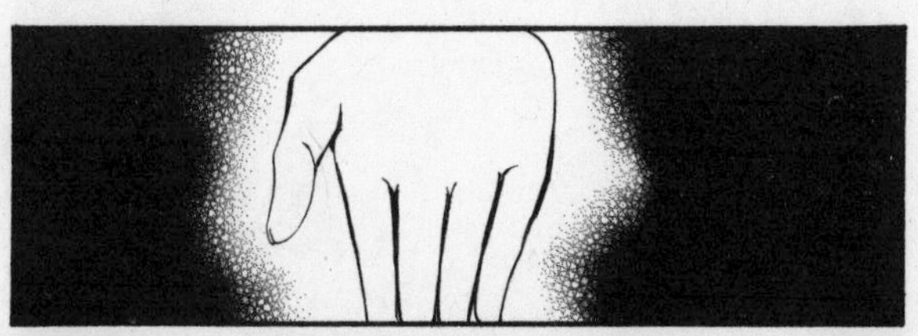

ZERO.
HAND OVER YOU-KNOW-WHAT.

HUH?
AH. BLOOD?
NO! WELL, I'D LIKE THAT TOO, BUT...
WHAT ARE YOU TALKING ABOUT?
THE EXCHANGE DIARY!
This is the back cover!
It's a squirrel!
Zero and Ai's Exchange Diary
DON'T READ IT!
I CAUGHT A GLIMPSE OF THIS AND GOT A BAD FEELING...
I WAS RIGHT !!
ALL MY EMBAR-RASSING SOLILOQUIES ARE IN HERE!
SHE EVEN WROTE THE COLOR OF MY UNDER-WEAR!
ACK...
AND THE TIME I WORE A PAIR INSIDE OUT.
MOMMY, HAVE I DONE SOMETHING BAD?
NO.

I NEVER KNEW YOU WERE ABLE TO WRITE SUCH GOOD SENTENCES, AI.
I'M SO HAPPY...
MOMMY!
AI!!
I'M TAKING A NAP...
YAWN
ZERO.
NOW THAT YOU'VE DISCOV- ERED MY SECRETS...
...I CAN'T ALLOW YOU TO LEAVE UNTIL WE'VE HAD A CHAT.
?
NAP...
AI, CAN YOU READ YOUR BOOK HERE BY YOURSELF?
OF COURSE I CAN!
GOOD GIRL!

WELL THEN...
...ZERO.
YES?

YOU KNEW IT ALL, BUT YOU DIDN'T TELL ME...
DON'T YOU THINK THAT WAS AWFUL OF YOU?

AFTER READING HER ENTRY TODAY, I WAS PLANNING TO TELL AI TO WRITE ONLY ABOUT HERSELF.
ANYWAY, IT'S YOUR DAUGHTER'S DIARY. YOU COULD SNEAK A PEEK OF IT SOMEHOW, COULDN'T YOU?

URGH...
BUT IF I DID THAT, I'D BE READING YOUR ENTRIES TOO...
...AND I'D FEEL GUILTY.
IT'S PRIVATE...

I DON'T MIND IF YOU READ IT.

I DO.

WHY?

IF I READ IT...
...IT'D BE...
...BOTHERSOME.
URK
IN WHAT WAY?
YOU'RE THE ONE SCOLDING ME. WHY AREN'T YOU BEING MORE FORTHCOMING?
MRRRR
IF YOU DON'T TELL ME, I'LL TELL EVERYONE THAT YOU ATTENDED THE SOIRÉE WITH YOUR UNDERWEAR ON INSIDE OUT.
IT'S BECAUSE YOUR ENTRIES ARE PROBABLY ABOUT ME BEING CUTE AND HOW MUCH YOU LOVE ME, YOU IDIOT!!
YOU KNOW ME WELL, HUH...

...
I'M HOR-RIBLE.
I'M HAPPY WHEN YOU COME TO SEE ME...
...BUT I'M UNABLE TO RETURN YOUR FEELINGS RIGHT NOW.
I-

I KNOW.
I'M SORRY.
I KNOW YOUR HEART HASN'T MOVED ON FROM THAT DAY...
I HAVE NO INTENTION OF RUSHING YOU.
I JUST WANTED YOU TO KNOW...
...THAT...
...MY FEELINGS HAVEN'T CHANGED.

YOU'RE...

...FREE TO LEAVE ME WHENEVER YOU DON'T NEED ME ANYMORE...

...

I COULD NEVER...

...LEAVE YOU.

I ONLY EVER WANT...

...YOUR BLOOD.

FOR A LONG TIME, YOU TOO...

...HAVEN'T DRUNK BLOOD OTHER THAN MINE.

I'M FORCING MYSELF TO BELIEVE THAT IT'S ONLY BECAUSE YOU FIND MY BLOOD VERY APPETIZING...
...UNTIL THE DAY YOU'RE READY TO ACCEPT THAT YOU'RE OBSESSED WITH ME.
ZERO...
I HAVE READ THE ENTRIES...
...IN THE FRONT OF THE DIARY.
"EVER SINCE YOU WERE BORN, AI, YOUR MOTHER HAS BEEN SMILING A LOT MORE."

"THAT MAKES ME HAPPY."
YOU WROTE THAT.
YEAH...
I WROTE THAT.
I'M GLAD...
...AI WAS BORN.

ME TOO.
THANK YOU FOR BEING WITH ME...
...ZERO.
I WANTED TO LET THE FLOW OF TIME SETTLE IT...
...BUT...

NOT EVERY-ONE WAS WILLING TO LET US SPEND THAT TIME IN PEACE.
LET US TALK ABOUT WHAT WE CLASSIFY AS ABNORMAL CRIMES...
RECENTLY WE HAVE DISCOVERED THE EXISTENCE OF A SPECIES KNOWN AS VAMPIRES. THEY HAVE THE DESIRE TO DRINK HUMAN BLOOD.
TO WHAT EXTENT CAN WE APPLY OUR CURRENT LAWS TO THIS SPECIES?
TO WHAT EXTENT CAN DRINKING HUMAN BLOOD FALL UNDER THEIR RIGHT TO EXIST?
OUR CURRENT LAWS ARE NOT COMPLEX ENOUGH, SO LET'S KEEP THAT IN MIND.
FIRST LET'S DISCUSS THE INFORMATION WE DO KNOW ABOUT THEM. YES, YOU...
THEY HAVE INCREDIBLE PHYSICAL ABILITIES, AND HUNTERS WHO SPECIALIZE IN BRINGING CRIMINAL VAMPIRES TO JUSTICE HAVE EXISTED FOR A WHILE.

YOU IN THE BACK.
THEY'RE NOCTURNAL.
UNLIKE THE LEGENDS, THEY DON'T TURN TO DUST WHEN THEY STAND IN THE SUN.
THEY LIKE THE SHADE.
YOU THERE. WHAT DID YOU WANT TO ADD?
THEY ARE NOT AFFLICTED BY AN ILLNESS. THEY ARE JUST LIKE HUMANS EXCEPT FOR THAT TRAIT.
OKAY, NEXT?
WE SHOULD TALK ABOUT THE MODEL CROSS ACADEMY SET FOR US.
EX-ACTLY.
HEY, CHECK OUT THAT GUY IN THE BACK WEARING THE PARKA.
IS HE AUDITING THIS CLASS?
HE'S PERFECTLY PROTECTED FROM THE SUN, SO HE MIGHT BE A VAMPIRE.
NO WAY... THOUGH I GUESS IT'S A POSSI-BILITY.
...
...
A SPECIES LIKE MANKIND—EXACTLY. WE ARE GRADUALLY PREPARING SOCIETY TO ACCEPT THEM INTO OUR COMMUNITY AS BEING JUST SLIGHTLY DIFFERENT FROM US.
BUT LIKE US, THERE ARE A FEW AMONG THEM WHO ARE VICIOUS CRIMINALS.
THE GOVERN-MENT HAS CONTINUED TO DELAY DISCLOSING ALL THE INFORMA-TION...

THERE YOU ARE, SHADY!
YOU ALWAYS DISAPPEAR SO QUICKLY AFTER CLASS.
WOULD YOU LIKE TO GO GET SOME TEA AFTER THIS?
...AWAY.
WHAT?
SORRY, WHAT DID YOU SAY?
LEAVE.
NOW.
TMP
OH.
I'M SORRY...

SO KIND...
YOU DROVE THE WEAKLING AWAY FROM DANGER.
YOU WANTED TO TALK TO ME, RIGHT?
I'M GLAD YOU'RE QUICK TO GET TO THE MATTER AT HAND...
...ZERO KIRYU.
I REQUEST THAT YOU DO NOT SEE YUKI-SAMA ANYMORE.

YOU ARE NOT SUITABLE...
...FOR OUR PUREBLOOD PRINCESS.
ARE YOU AN ACQUAINTANCE OF YUKI'S?
I HAVEN'T SEEN YOU BEFORE.
I BECAME A SUPPORTER OF YUKI-SAMA AFTER SEEING HER AT THE SOIRÉE.
I AM NOTHING BUT A PEBBLE ON THE STREET TO HER.
RELATIONS BETWEEN THE HUNTER SOCIETY AND VAMPIRES HAVE IMPROVED, BUT THAT IS OF NO CONSEQUENCE.
YOU ARE ONE WHO WIELDS A WEAPON TO SLAY US.
I WOULD LIKE YOU TO STOP TAINTING YUKI-SAMA WITH THOSE DIRTY HANDS OF YOURS.

I CAN'T DO THAT.

THEN DIE!

ONLY YUKI AND AI...
...CAN TAKE AWAY MY RIGHT TO BE WITH HER.
CROSSING
Rose

FWAA
YUKI...
ZERO...
...WAS ATTACKED AGAIN.

WHAT THAT MAN SAID...
ZERO ISN'T TAINTED AT ALL.
AND THAT MAN WASN'T...
...THE ONLY ONE...

SORRY, AI.
YOUR MOM...
...WILL BE BUSIER FROM NOW ON.
LEAVE...
...ZERO.

I DON'T WANT TO SEE YOUR FACE FOR A WHILE.

MRRR

I'M REALLY ANGRY RIGHT NOW.
THERE ARE SO MANY STUPID PEOPLE WHO WON'T UNDER-STAND UNLESS I TELL THEM.
YUKI WENT AROUND MAKING THREATS.
SHE ORDERED THEM NOT TO LAY A HAND ON ME.

MEAN-WHILE, I TOO...
I'M WILLING TO ACCEPT THAT YOU'RE FRIENDS WITH THE BOSS OF THE VAMPIRES AND THAT YOU DRINK HER BLOOD.
RIGHT. AFTER ALL, WE HUNTERS STRADDLE THE LINE BETWEEN VAMPIRES AND HUMANS.
BUT IF THE FUTURE LEADER OF THE HUNTER SOCIETY WERE TO HAVE A PUREBLOOD WIFE...
...THAT MIGHT WEAR DOWN OUR MORALE, YOU KNOW? WE'D BE THE SUBORDINATE OFFICERS OF A PUREBLOOD'S HUSBAND.
WE THOUGHT YOU HATED PUREBLOODS MORE THAN ANYONE.
...WAS SECRETLY FIGHTING...
...A MODEST BATTLE.
THE WARMTH OF THE PRINCESS OF MY MEMORIES/END

HAKAMORI...?
KONOE!
VAMPIRE KNIGHT
MEMORIES
STARS THAT SHINE IN DARKNESS

OOH...
WHAT SHOULD I HAVE HER WEAR?!
RUKA...?
IT'S A RARE CHANCE FOR ME TO CHOOSE WHAT AI-SAMA WILL WEAR.

IT'S PURE HAPPINESS TO PICK OUT CLOTHES FOR YOU, AI-SAMA. YOU LOOK SO MUCH LIKE KANAME-SAMA...
...WHEN I MET HIM FOR THE VERY FIRST TIME!!
I'LL PUT YOU IN FEMALE UNDER-GARMENTS AND CLOTHES. TIGHTS... AND A RIBBON!
AAH... I MUSTN'T INDULGE IN OLD FANTASIES...
IF YOU LOVE DRESSING UP CHILDREN, WHY DON'T YOU MAKE ONE...
...WITH M—
P
GURK
OOM
GET OUT!!
YOU'RE IN FRONT OF AN INFANT!
SLAM!!
GUGH...

WHERE ARE WE GOING?
TO A PLACE DEEP IN THE FOREST OF CROSS ACADEMY... A DORM THAT IS NO LONGER IN USE.
YOUR MOTHER WILL COME THERE LATER, SO DON'T WORRY.
YOUR MOTHER MUST LEAVE YOU FOR A LITTLE WHILE TO DO SOME THINGS...
...SO SHE WANTED YOU TO LIVE SOMEWHERE SAFE.
CROSS ACADEMY...
THAT'S THE PLACE WHERE DADDY KANAME IS SLEEPING IN THE BASEMENT.
THERE'S A NICE PARFAIT SHOP NEARBY.
IT'S NEAR DADDY ZERO'S WORKPLACE.
IT'S FAR FROM THE UNIVER-SITY...
THAT'S RIGHT.
AN IMPORTANT FURNACE IS IN THE BASEMENT...
...AND BECAUSE OF THAT, THE HUNTER SOCIETY'S NEW HEADQUARTERS WAS BUILT NEAR THERE.
THE ANCESTOR METAL IN THAT FURNACE WILL KEEP AWAY ANY MALICIOUS VAMPIRES.

AND SO—

PLEASE CHANGE INTO THIS!

IT'S SLIGHTLY BOYISH. ♡

SHINING☆

WEL-
COME...
OUR PURE-
BLOOD
PRINCESS...

THE LAST TIME I SAW YOU WAS AT THAT SOIRÉE IN WINTER, BUT YOU HAVE NOT CHANGED AT ALL...
WHAT BRINGS YOU TO MY HUMBLE ESTABLISH-MENT TONIGHT?
YESTERDAY IN THE EARLY EVENING, A FOOL ATTACKED ZERO KIRYU.
IF HE HAD NOT TRIED TO DO SOMETHING IDIOTIC, HIS LIFE WOULD HAVE BEEN SPARED...
HE WAS YOUR SERVANT...
...RIGHT?
I DID NOT...
...ORDER HIM TO DO THAT.
I BEG YOUR PARDON, OUR YOUNG PUREBLOOD HIGHNESS.

I DO NOT KNOW ABOUT THE PEOPLE WHO SERVE AT YOUR SIDE...
...BUT NONE OF US DESIRE TO SEE YOU AND THAT HUNTER HAPPILY UNITED.
PLEASE CHOOSE A PUREBLOOD MALE AS YOUR PARTNER.
I HOPE...
...YOU'RE NOT SAYING THIS IS THE CONDI-TION...
...FOR YOUR ALLEGIANCE TO ME...

NO, YOUR HIGHNESS... OUR LOYALTY IS OF LITTLE WORTH TO YOU.
JUST LIKE A MOTH DRAWN TO A FLAME, WE ARE BORN WITH THIS TRAIT AND ARE UNABLE TO RESIST YOU...
...THOUGH WE REGARD IT AS A BLESSING.
MAY I HAVE A WORD TOO, YUKI-SAMA?
WATCH YOUR MANNERS!
WHAT IS IT?
UM, BASICALLY...
MANY OF US BELIEVE THAT OUR ARCHENEMY WILL END UP IMPREGNATING OUR PRECIOUS AND BELOVED PUREBLOOD.
WE CANNOT PERMIT THAT, SO WE'RE GONNA KICK UP A FUSS TO STOP IT.

HOLD YOUR TONGUE!
THAT'S TOO BAD.
CHOOSING THAT PATH...

...WILL ONLY LEAD TO YOU GETTING KILLED BY EITHER ZERO OR ME.
DON'T WASTE YOUR LIVES ON A FRUITLESS ENDEAVOR.
THAT'S ALL I CAME TO SAY.

BREAK IT OFF.
PLEASE!
I'M SORRY, BUT...
NEVER...
...I WILL NOT REJECT YUKI AGAIN.
...NO MATTER WHAT.

I ADMIT...
...I HAVE A REASON TO HATE VAMPIRES...AND THE PUREBLOODS. I HATE THEM SO MUCH THAT I CAN'T...
...HATE THEM ENOUGH.
SO I UNDERSTAND YOUR MIXED FEELINGS.
THEN ...?
YOU DON'T KNOW...
...HOW IT FEELS...
...TO TRULY STARVE.

THAT'S...
...
IF IT EVER HAPPENS AGAIN, I KNOW I'M NOT STRONG ENOUGH...
...TO ENDURE IT.

I'M OFF.

IF YOU DON'T THINK I'M SUITED TO BECOME THE NEXT LEADER OF THE HUNTER SOCIETY, TELL THAT TO THE CURRENT PRESIDENT.

WAIT. WE'RE NOT DONE YET...

I DON'T CARE WHAT HAPPENS AS LONG AS MY WEAPON ISN'T TAKEN AWAY.

ZERO!

ISN'T THE TERM "VAMPIRE" DEROGA-TORY?
THEY MAY BE BLESSED WITH VARIOUS POWERS...
...BUT THEY ARE FOREVER UNABLE TO FEEL THE WARM SUN, AND THEY STRUGGLE WITH EATING DISORDERS. THEY ARE BURDENED WITH A HEREDITARY DISEASE—
I SEE. THEN—
FOR THE TIME BEING THEY WON'T PUBLICIZE THE FACT THAT CERTAIN VAMPIRES ARE ABLE TO INFECT HUMANS WITH THEIR DISEASE.
THE PURE-BLOODS HAVE AGREED TO LIE LOW, SO IT SHOULD BE OKAY.
WELL...
I HEAR THERE ARE VAMPIREPHILES WHO HAVE INFLUENCED PEOPLE TO COME FORTH TO DONATE BLOOD.
YEAH...
WELL, FOR A PRIME EXAMPLE OF A VAMPIREPHILE, WE NEED ONLY LOOK...

...TO OUR PRESIDENT.

THANK YOU VERY MUCH FOR YOUR SUPPORT...

...CON-GRESSMAN WAKABA.

OH NO, CROSS.

I'M ONLY DOING THIS BECAUSE I INTEND...

...TO MAKE USE OF THEIR ABILITIES IN THE FUTURE.

BUT YOUR HONESTY HAS MORE WORTH THAN THE WORDS OF A RECKLESS PHILANTHRO-PIST.

—2—

(continued ↓)

In volume 2 I feel that I have been able to place the characters in a gentle flow of time for the first time in the *Vampire Knight* series.

(Although time is really flying by in the story...?)

By the way, I recently realized that I hardly ever abbreviate the title of this series in my conversations and emails. The only time I do is when I write VK (VKM for this series) for the folder and file illustration names. But I received a letter that had "Vamp Knight," and...

(continues ↓)

PUTTING THAT ASIDE...
...WHAT IS HANABUSA AIDO LIKE AS A PERSON?
WELL...
YOU'LL UNDERSTAND ONCE YOU MEET HIM A COUPLE OF TIMES.
OF COURSE YOU DON'T WANT YOUR DAUGHTER TO GO THROUGH HARDSHIP.
I UNDERSTAND HOW YOU FEEL.
BECAUSE OF HER BLOOD-LINE...
...MY DAUGHTER TOO HAS FACED DIFFICULT TIMES.

IT...
...WOULDN'T BE AN OVER-STATEMENT...
...TO SAY THAT I AM DOING ALL THIS BECAUSE I WANT HER TO BE FREE.

FWOOM
!
OOPS...
ZISH

—3—

(continued ↓)

...I happened to read that part out loud...

Vamp Knight
↑
M
M
B
L

HINO

*I wasn't sure if the Knight part was meant to be abbreviated or not.

...and I was filled with a strange embarrassed feeling. But then again, it really isn't much to talk about.

Anyway, let me get back to the matter at hand.

I was not intending *Memories* to become a continuing series when I started it, so some of the chapters in volume 2 are set in the same timeline as volume 1.

(continues ↓)

ARE YOU OKAY, HANABUSA?!

YOU'RE HURT—

I'M FINE. I'M FINE.

I'M GOOD AT CONTROLLING HEAT JUST LIKE AKATSUKI.

SEE?

I'M UN-HARMED.

YOU'RE RIGHT...

...

?

WHAT IS IT, HANABUSA?

...
VEEN
WHAT?
SWIP
SWIP
PSST
IF YOU WANT TO KISS ME...
...IT'S ALL RIGHT.

BLUSH
HUH?
W-WHAT ARE YOU SAYING?!
HA HA HA HA HA!
SWIP SWIP
SWIP
I...
...THOUGHT YOU SEEMED A LITTLE DOWN. I WAS MERELY TRYING TO OBSERVE YOU... MORE...
WHAT?

THAT'S PROBABLY BECAUSE YOU CARE ABOUT MY FEELINGS.
I CAN'T HELP BUT BELIEVE THAT.
R...
REALLY ...?
REALLY.
I LOOKED UP AND THOUGHT THE SKY WAS...
...EXCEP-TIONALLY BEAUTIFUL TONIGHT.
THEN I WONDERED IF I HAD EVER BEEN MOVED THIS MUCH BY LOOKING AT A STARRY SKY...
...IN THE PAST.

I FEEL THIS WAY...
...BECAUSE YOU'RE HERE, HANABUSA. I'M VERY HAPPY...
THAT'S WHY THE NIGHT SKY SEEMS SO MUCH MORE BEAUTIFUL THAN BEFORE.
AND I'VE DECIDED TO STOP WORRYING ABOUT GETTING MARRIED.
AFTER ALL, YOU CARE FOR ME...
...AND THAT WON'T CHANGE.

WAKABA.
I'LL ACCOMPANY YOU DOWN TO THE STATION, SO WOULD YOU JOIN ME ON A LITTLE WALK?
BOW
PHOO.
ARE YOU SURE?
DO YOU THINK OF ME AS AN INFLEXIBLE GUY WHO DOESN'T KNOW WHAT TO PRIORITIZE?
...
SO YOU DO...
I'M SORRY.
I CAN'T GIVE YOU AN IMMEDIATE ANSWER.
I KNOW THAT HUMAN TIME...
...IS VERY PRECIOUS, BUT...

NO...
IT'S OKAY.
I'VE COME TO UNDERSTAND YOUR IDIOSYN-CRASY ABOUT NOT GETTING MARRIED BEFORE THE ONE YOU SERVE.
MY IDIOSYN-CRASY, HUH.
YOU'RE RIGHT.
IT IS BEAUTIFUL.
WHEN I'M WITH YOU LIKE THIS, WAKABA...
...THE STARS TRULY ARE BEAUTIFUL.
THE MORE...
...I THINK ABOUT IT...

...YOU'RE THE ONLY ONE...
...I CAN SHARE THIS WITH.
MAY I...
HUH?
MAY I PUT MY ARM AROUND YOUR SHOULDERS?!
RAPT
YES...
OKAY!
HEE
WHIP
SUFF

THERE.
AND...
!
ZISH
URGH.
ARE YOU ALL RIGHT?
GRIP
SHE'S A VAMPIRE.

YOU MUST BE THE ELDEST SON OF THE AIDO FAMILY. HANABUSA-SAMA...?
PLEASE HELP ME.
A HUNTER ATTACKED ME FOR NO LEGITIMATE REASON—
THSH
YANK
...?!
IF WE CAN'T DO ANYTHING ABOUT OUR HIGHNESS'S CHOICE, WE'LL TAKE ADVANTAGE OF HER WEAKNESSES!
HA HA HA HA HA

KREK
KRSSH
THUD

WHO THE HELL...
...ARE YOU?
THAT HARDLY MATTERS NOW!
WE'VE ACCOM-PLISHED WHAT WE CAME HERE FOR!
DASH
WE NEEDED ONLY TO THREATEN YOU!
VUMP
MAY OUR PUREBLOOD PRINCESS—
KREEK

SHUNK
ARE YOU ALL RIGHT?!
YOU'RE NOT HURT?
ARE THEY...?
THEY'RE FINE.
THEY WON'T DIE UNLESS THEIR BODIES ARE SHATTERED.
I...
I'M ALL RIGHT. MY HEART IS BEATING REALLY FAST, BUT...
YOU'RE SURE YOU'RE OKAY?!
WHAT WAS THAT...
...ABOUT THREATEN-ING US?
DON'T WORRY ABOUT THAT NOW.
GRIP
SORRY.
I WAS RIGHT BESIDE YOU TOO...

I WAS DISTRACTED. I WAS THINKING ONLY ABOUT YOU...
I THOUGHT...
"IF IT'S WAKABA... NO, IT HAS TO BE WAKABA..."
"WHAT I WANT TO CHERISH...
"...IS MY TIME WITH HER."
I ONLY REALIZED WHAT HAPPINESS IS AFTER BEING WITH YOU.

YOU TOLD ME WHY YOU FELL IN LOVE WITH ME... REMEMBER?
IT MADE ME INCREDIBLY HAPPY.
NOW IT'S MY TURN.
I'M GOING TO FOLLOW MY TRUE FEELINGS.
SAYORI...
...WAKABA...

WILL YOU BECOME MY WIFE?
...
YES...

I'M GLAD TO HEAR YOU RECEIVED SUCH GOOD NEWS.
UH-HUH!
HOW DO YOU FEEL ABOUT IT, ZERO?
OF COURSE I'M HAPPY TOO.

STARS THAT SHINE IN DARKNESS/END

VAMPIRE
KNIGHT
MEMORIES

THE BOX IN THE DEPTHS OF ONE'S SOUL THAT MUST NOT BE OPENED

EXCUSE ME...
YOU THERE.
THIS IS NO PLACE TO BE WALKING AROUND LATE AT NIGHT.
YOU SHOULD GO HOME BEFORE YOU SLIP AND FALL.
...
OH...?

IS IT POSSIBLE...
...YOU'RE—
DON'T GET ANY CLOSER TO HIM...
...VAMPIRE WOMAN.
PLEASE TELL ME WHY YOU'VE COME HERE.
OTHERWISE...
WHAT...? I-I'M NOT... I ONLY...
REN.
LET THE WOMAN GO.
I DON'T SENSE ANY ANIMOSITY FROM HER.

FORGIVE MY FAMILY MEMBER'S RUDENESS.
BUT DO FORGET THIS NIGHT.
AH...
MY LADY...
FORGET...
...AND DON'T ENTER THIS AREA AGAIN.
YES...
AS YOU SAY...
TMP
TMP
TMP
GLARE

I DON'T MIND WHERE YOU GO AT NIGHT BECAUSE I'LL PROTECT YOU NO MATTER WHAT!
AND I'M SURE YOU WANT TO WANDER OFF BECAUSE YOU'VE LOST YOUR MEMORY!
BUT YOU WALKED AROUND FOR THREE HOURS, AND THEN YOU JUST STOOD IN THIS SAME SPOT FOR HALF AN HOUR! ARGH!
WHAT'S HE DOING?
TEP TEP
WHAT IS HE UP TO?!
LOST IN THOUGHT
YOU...
...
IT DIDN'T SEEM ODD TO ME, BUT...
...I'M SORRY I WORRIED YOU.

THE SMELL OF GRASS AND EARTH...
THE COLD NIGHT BREEZE ON MY CHEEKS...
THEN I NOTICED A CURTAIN OF DROPS OF LIGHT...
...CASCADING THROUGH THE CANOPY OF TREES.

THIS MIGHT BE THE FIRST TIME IN MY LIFE...
...I'VE FELT THE COMFORT OF THESE BREATHING STARS...
...DEEP WITHIN MY ENTIRE BODY.

I DON'T REMEMBER, OF COURSE...
...BUT THAT'S THE FEELING I HAVE.
REN...
THERE'S A SCRATCH ON YOUR CHEEK.
KLUP
SWUP
OH...
I'M FINE.
I DIDN'T BOTHER AVOIDING A BRANCH.
MY WOUND HAS ALREADY HEALED.
THAT WAS MY FAULT. I'M SORRY...

NO...
LET'S GO HOME.
TOMORROW I WANT TO SHOW YOU THE TOWN YOU CAN SEE FROM HERE.
A VAMPIRE'S POWER OF REGENERA-TION...

IF I TORE HER OUT OF MY BODY...
...WOULD SHE RE-GENERATE?

DO YOU WANT TO TRY?
WHAT ARE YOU SAYING, AI?!
I...
...WAS NOT SURPRISED NOR FRIGHTENED THAT HE ASKED THAT.
I FELT NO DREAD...
...OR DANGER.
I FELT NOTHING.

BECAUSE I KNEW...

LET'S NOT.

I HAVE A FEELING I WOULD BE SCOLDED TERRIBLY...

...BY HER.

I DON'T THINK IT WAS...
...STUPID.
...WHAT IS CARVED INTO THIS PERSON'S SOUL.
GRIP
I...
...LEARNT THAT FROM MY MOTHER.

I DO NOT REGRET IT NOW.

BUT BACK THEN, I REGRETTED IT SO MUCH THAT I WANTED TO DECOMPOSE INTO PARTICLES...

AI, YOUR HAIR...

...IS A LOT LIKE YOUR FATHER'S.

IT FEELS SO GOOD TO THE TOUCH.

DADDY KANAME?

YES.

YOU TAKE AFTER HIM...

GLOOM

YOU DON'T SMELL LIKE HIM, THOUGH...

SNIFF SNIFF

DON'T SNIFF ME!

YOU'RE SO CUTE.
I LOVE YOU...
...MY PRECIOUS DAUGHTER.
MM...
I...
...LOVE YOU TOO.
DO YOU LOVE DADDY KANAME?
OF COURSE.
THEN WHAT ABOUT...
Z—
HEY! YOU TWO BETTER BE READY BECAUSE WE HAVE TO GO!
WE'RE COMING!

—4—

(continued ↓)

I may even go far back into the past again in order to shine the spotlight on a different character in volume 3. The time keeps flowing back and forth into the past and future in *Memories* because of the creator's selfishness, but I hope you will keep watching over me with kind eyes.

By the way, I wrote "future" above, but I think it would be more correct to say "present" in this case...

The time since the moment Kaname awoke at the end of volume 19 is the actual present.

(continues ↓)

YOU LOOK CUTE...
...AI.
GOOD LUCK...
...WITH YOUR FIRST SOIRÉE.

LITTLE PRIN- CESS...
...IT IS AN HONOR TO HAVE YOU AT MY HUMBLE GATH—
DON'T YOU TOUCH ME!
GURK
WILL YOU GIVE ME THE HONOR OF THIS DANCE—
YOUR FACE IS TOO CLOSE!!
GYAAH
SOB SOB
I'M SORRY...
I'M SO SORRY, EVERYONE...
SOB SOB
SOB SOB
NOT AT ALL.

I'M THE ONE WHO WANTED TO COME...
I'M SORRY...
SORRY, EVERY-ONE...
YOU CAN ACCEPT ANOTHER INVITATION ONCE YOU'VE GOTTEN A LITTLE BIGGER.
I DON'T REALLY ENJOY SOIRÉES EITHER, SO YOU DON'T NEED TO FORCE YOURSELF.
MOTHER...
YOU'D RATHER BE AT A SOIRÉE WITH ME THAN ON YOUR OWN, RIGHT?
AI...
WHAT'S WRONG?
DID SOME-THING HAPPEN?

—5—

(continued ↓)

I chose to call this series *Memories* because I wanted to write about the memories of the past from that point in the story. I may sound like I'm saying something grand, but basically I'm being very picky, that's all.

Maybe—this is something that may happen in the future—I might get the chance to focus on a certain character and write about the "behind the scenes" world of *Vampire Knight* from that character's perspective. Like I said, it's a "maybe," so it could turn out to be a "maybe not."

(continues ↓)

ARE YOU ALL RIGHT...?
GRIP
SHE...
...PUSHED HERSELF TOO HARD.
I SEE.
COME ON.
LET'S GO HOME.

IF THEY WERE YOU, ZERO...
...I WOULD'VE BEEN HAPPY TO BE TOUCHED BY THEM...
HUG
SOB
BYE.
YUKI.

NEXT TIME I WANT TO SEE YOU IN A PROPER DRESS.
BLEAAH
DADDY ZERO...
...HASN'T SLEPT OVER AT OUR PLACE FOR LONG TIME.
ARE YOU BOTH TOO BUSY?
HM.
THAT TOO...
BUT WE DECIDED IT WOULD BE BETTER THIS WAY FOR NOW.

THERE ARE...
...MANY REASONS.
LISTEN...
...MOTHER.
IF YOU DON'T NEED ZERO ANYMORE...
MAY I...

?
WHAT'S THE MATTER, AI?
SHALL WE GO INSIDE?
HOW CAN I EVEN ASK THAT?!
BUT... I KNOW...
AH. UM...
I CAN...
...ASK HER IN AN INDIRECT WAY.
M...
MOTHER.
IS ZERO ANGRY AT YOU BECAUSE YOU STILL LOVE DADDY KANAME?!

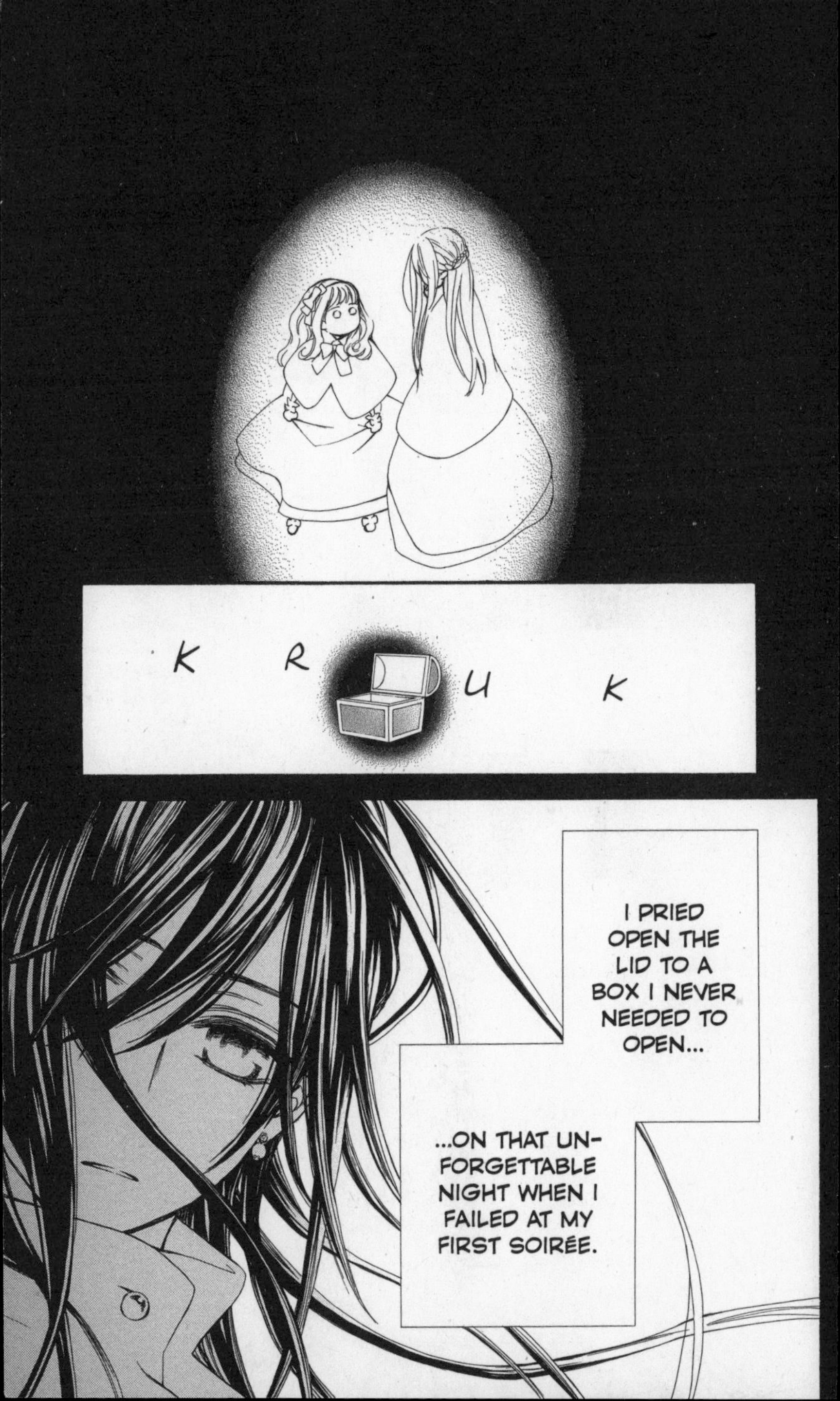

K R U K
I PRIED OPEN THE LID TO A BOX I NEVER NEEDED TO OPEN...
...ON THAT UN-FORGETTABLE NIGHT WHEN I FAILED AT MY FIRST SOIRÉE.

I STOOD IN FRONT OF THE COFFIN OF ICE THAT ENCASED HIM...
...AND I DIDN'T SLEEP OR EAT. I JUST STAYED THERE THINKING FOR A LONG TIME.
ZERO WOULD BE THE BIGGEST THREAT AND GREATEST OBSTACLE.
BUT IF I USED THE NEWLY CREATED VAMPIRE HUNTER WEAPON TO RID THE WORLD OF ALL VAMPIRES...
...THERE WOULD BE NO REASON FOR HIM TO REMAIN SLEEPING INSIDE THAT COFFIN OF ICE.
AND I HAD THE POWER TO DO THAT...
...YOU SEE.

I HAD NEVER SEEN MY MOTHER LOOK SO TERRIFYING.
YOU SAVED ME...
...FROM THAT TERRIBLE DARKNESS.

ZERO...
...AND YOU, THE CHILD KANAME GAVE ME.
SOON AFTER...
...I WOULD LEARN THE STORY OF WHAT HAPPENED BETWEEN MY MOTHER, ZERO, AND KANAME.
THE BOX IN THE DEPTHS OF ONE'S SOUL THAT MUST NOT BE OPENED/END

VAMPIRE
KNIGHT
MEMORIES
AI AND HER FIRST LOVE

THAT STORY WAS LOVING...
I WANT YOU TO BE TOGETHER...

...AND
PASSIONATE
AND SAD.
FOOM

WHEN YOU WERE STILL INSIDE ME...
MY MOTHER SOUNDED KIND AS SHE SPOKE.
...ZERO AND I WITNESSED THE BIRTH OF THE FIRST ANTI-VAMPIRE WEAPONS FROM THE FURNACE...
...HIS HEART HAD MELTED INTO.
WE BOTH WERE EXPECTING SOMETHING SPECIAL TO HAPPEN...

...BUT
WHAT USED
TO BE HIS
CORE...
...ONLY
EXISTED
THERE TO
BESTOW
WEAPONS
WITH THE
POWER TO
KILL
VAMPIRES.

WE CAN FORGET ABOUT THE VAMPIRES WHO THREATEN THE LIVES OF HUMANS...
...AND SIMPLY TAKE OUT KANAME KURAN'S HEART FROM THE FURNACE.
B-BMP
OR WE COULD USE EVERYTHING WE'VE GOT TO KILL EVERY VAMPIRE AND PLACE HIS HEART BACK INTO HIS BODY IMMEDI-ATELY AFTER.
THEN WE COULD MAKE HIM CLEAR UP THE MESS HE LEFT BEHIND.

I THOUGHT OF THAT...
...BUT IT'S WRONG, ISN'T IT?
LEAVING A WORLD LIKE THAT FOR THE LITTLE ONE INSIDE YOU...
...TO GROW UP IN...
...ISN'T RIGHT.
...

YES...
I KNOW.
SO IN THE END, EVERYTHING IS THE WAY HE WANTED IT TO BE.
HE REALLY IS SUCH AN ANNOYING GUY.

CAN YOU ACCEPT...

...THIS SIGHT IN FRONT OF YOU?

I DON'T KNOW...

BUT...

...I'M...

...PREPARED TO FACE IT.

AND SO... THAT'S PRETTY MUCH IT FOR THE STORY ABOUT ME, ZERO, AND YOUR FATHER, KANAME.
OKAY...
I'VE LEFT OUT THE PARTS THAT ARE TOO DIFFICULT OR CAN'T BE EXPLAINED TO YOU JUST YET...
I'LL TELL YOU ABOUT THOSE ONCE YOU'VE GROWN UP.
THERE ARE MANY THINGS I STILL HAVEN'T BEEN ABLE TO COME TO TERMS WITH MYSELF.
THE REASON I LIVE ON...
...IS BECAUSE I HAVE SOMEONE I WANT TO PROTECT RIGHT HERE, AI.
PWUB
AND I HAVE SOME-ONE...
...WHOM I CAN TRUST TO PROTECT MY BACK, AND WHO SOMETIMES FACES THE SAME DIRECTION AND HAS THE SAME FEELINGS I DO.
MY MOTHER ADDED THAT AT THE END AFTER TELLING ME WHAT HAD HAPPENED IN THE PAST.

AND...

...I REALIZED THAT I REGRETTED KNOWING...

...WHAT HAD HAPPENED AMONG THEM IN THE PAST...

PWUB

YOU MEAN ZERO...

ACK!

GYAAAAAH

TMP TMP

WHY DIDN'T ANYONE WAKE ME?!

UURGH

I HAVE A MEETING TODAY!

BAM

I DID.
YOU ANSWERED ME.
YOU'RE LIKE A CHILD, HANA.
SO EMBAR-RASSING...
DID YOU WANT ME TO WAKE YOU UP...?
HI, WE'RE HERE TOO.
WHAT ARE THESE TWO NUISANCES DOING HERE?
YUKI SAID SHE WOULD GIVE US THE BABY STROLLER SHE HAD USED, SO THEY BROUGHT IT HERE FOR US.
OH...
BLUSH
I REMEMBER NOW.
I DID HEAR ABOUT THAT YESTERDAY.
YOU DON'T HAVE MUCH TIME, SO I'LL PREPARE SOMETHING YOU CAN EAT QUICKLY.
AH
OOF.
GET READY WHILE I MAKE IT.
NO, WAIT!
IT'S TIME YOU STARTED RELYING ON OUR HOUSE-KEEPER TO COOK NOW.
BUT I'M STILL FINE.
NO!

—6—

(continued ↓)

Let me return to the main subject...

It would take a while longer for me to begin focusing on the actions of Kaname after he has become a human. But I hope to include tidbits about his ~~comedic life~~ strange life with Ai and Ren.

And...

I did say this series would supplement the final chapter of volume 19, but I would like to write the fateful arcs of the other characters, which I was unable to do during volumes 1–19.

Thus...

I would also write about the unavoidable incident.

(continues ↓)

TOO MUCH CHEEK, KIRYU!
IT'S ABOUT TIME I TAUGHT YOU A LESSON!
COME OUT-SIDE!
HUH?
WHAT A PAIN...
HANA IS SO KIND TO YOU, YORI.
HEE HEE
I'M PROUD TO HAVE HIM AS MY HUSBAND.
YORI...
...YOU LOVE HANA TOO.
YES.
THAT'S WHY I'M SO HAPPY I MARRIED HANABUSA.
...
WHAT'S WRONG?
UM...
BEFORE...
...YOU WERE MARRIED...

DID YOU FEEL HAPPY WHEN HANA PATTED YOU ON THE HEAD?
WHAT?
WELL...
HE NEVER PATTED ME THAT MUCH, BUT...
I WAS HAPPY...
AND WHAT ABOUT WHEN HE HUGGED YOU TIGHTLY?
AI.

YES...
I WAS SO HAPPY THAT IT MADE MY HEART LEAP.
KRRK
AI.
WE'RE LEAVING NOW.
JOLT
WHY DO YOU ASK?
THOSE WERE VERY SPECIFIC QUES-TIONS.

BLUSH
BOW
BYE... I HOPE YOU GIVE BIRTH TO A HEALTHY BABY.
THANK YOU FOR HAVING ME.
ZERO, LET'S GO!
I'VE JUST DECIDED!
I'M TAKING SOME TIME OFF WORK!

PEEK
VEEN
SWIP
I REALIZED MY FEELINGS FOR HIM...
...ONE NIGHT WHEN I WAS EIGHT.

AI? DID I WAKE YOU UP?

WELCOME HOME. I WENT TO YORI'S PLACE TO DELIVER THE STROLLER.

YORI WAS SMILING THE WHOLE TIME.

I BET... THEY'RE SUCH A LOVING COUPLE, AREN'T THEY?
THANKS FOR DOING THAT.

UH-HUH...

UM...
HM?
AREN'T YOU... LONELY, MOTHER?
WHAT ARE YOU TALKING ABOUT?
HEH HEH
GO BACK TO SLEEP.
...
...

DASH
THE NEXT DAY, I MADE A DECISION.
ZERO.
I'M SORRY I'VE KEPT YOU WAITING IN THE GARDEN...
...AFTER CALLING YOU HERE AFTER WORK.
THAT'S OKAY.

I...
...HAVE SOMETHING SERIOUS TO DISCUSS.
GRIP

I...
...WANT TO BECOME YOUR WIFE SOMEDAY!

THEN I WILL ANSWER YOU SERIOUSLY TOO.
IF I WERE TO EVER TAKE A WIFE...
...SHE WOULD BE NO ONE ELSE BUT YUKI.

I'M SORRY...
...AI.
OKAY.
I KNOW.

WOULD YOU DANCE WITH ME?
I WOULD LIKE TO DANCE WITH THE ONE...
...I SHARED MY FEELINGS WITH TONIGHT.
TINK

ONLY UNTIL THE MUSIC BOX STOPS PLAYING.
I WANT THIS TO BE OUR SPECIAL TIME.
I'M SOMEONE WHO HUNTED DOWN ANOTHER VAMPIRE TODAY...
...BUT IF THAT DOESN'T BOTHER YOU...

THANK YOU...
...ZERO.
PLEASE DON'T TELL MOTHER, OKAY?
THAT NIGHT...

...I CAME TO TERMS WITH MY UNREQUITED FIRST LOVE BEFORE IT BEGAN TO HAUNT ME.
WHEN I WAS OLD ENOUGH TO UNDERSTAND THE EMOTIONS OF THOSE THREE PEOPLE, I REALIZED THAT DECISION WAS A TURNING POINT IN MY LIFE.
BECAUSE...
...THOSE FIRES IN MY HEART WOULD HAVE PROBABLY CONSUMED ME LONG BEFORE...
...I WOULD FIND MYSELF ONE NIGHT BEING MOVED BY THE BEAUTY OF A STARLIT SKY.

OKAY...
YOU TWO.

STOP BEING SO MELAN-CHOLY.
HAVE FUN TOGETHER AND CHEER UP!
BY THE WAY, I LIED ABOUT THERE BEING A GHOST IN THIS ROOM.

HURRY UP AND GET MARRIED, YOU IDIOTS!!
BAM!!
WHAT?
KA-CHAK
IDIOTS?
IS...
IS THIS HER REBEL-LIOUS AGE?!
SHE LOCKED THE DOOR...

SHOULD WE BREAK DOWN THE DOOR?

OR SHOULD WE WAIT FOR HER TO OPEN IT?

...IT WOULD TAKE THEM SEVERAL DECADES AFTER THIS.

AI AND HER FIRST LOVE/END

VAMPIRE KNIGHT
MEMORIES

YOU ARE MY NORTH STAR

AI.
I CANNOT ALLOW YOU TO GO OUTSIDE THIS HOUSE FOR SOME TIME.
IT'S SO THAT THERE WON'T BE ANY UNFORTUNATE VICTIMS... YOU UNDERSTAND, DON'T YOU?
OF COURSE.
I DON'T WANT TO DO ANYTHING SO PITIFUL LIKE SUDDENLY ATTACKING SOMEONE.
LOSING MY HEAD, HOLDING THEM DOWN AND BITING THEM...
...UNTIL THEY'VE LOST TOO MUCH BLOOD...
...AND TELLING THEM THEY'LL FOREVER REMAIN AS MY VAMPIRE SERVANT...

I DON'T WANT TO DO THINGS THAT PEOPLE WOULD HATE.
I DON'T WANT...
...TO BE DESPISED BY OTHERS.
YOU LOOK AWFUL.
I FEEL SO SORRY FOR YOU...
I...WANT MY FIRST PERSON TO BE YOU, MOTHER...
...SO PLEASE STAY NEAR ME.
OF COURSE.
DON'T LET THE HOUSE-KEEPERS COME NEAR ME.
I WON'T.
DON'T LET ANY MEN INSIDE THE HOUSE FOR A WHILE.
ALL RIGHT.

AI-SAMA, YOU ONLY NEED TO BEAR THIS FOR ABOUT A MONTH.

ONCE YOU GET PAST THIS UNSTABLE PERIOD, YOU WILL BECOME A FULL-FLEDGED VAMPIRE.

MY FIRST WAS MY MOTHER TOO.

SO FEEL FREE TO SINK YOUR TEETH INTO HER.

THAT WAY IT DOESN'T CREATE FUTURE PROBLEMS.

I UNDER-STAND WHAT YOU'RE GOING THROUGH...
...AI.
I KNOW THE ONE PERSON...
...YOU DON'T WANT TO BE DESPISED BY IS ZERO.
WHEN YOU CAME HOME CRYING ONE NIGHT...
...I UNDER-STOOD WHAT HAD HAPPENED.
YOUR FEELINGS FOR HIM WERE REAL...
...AND YOU HAD BROUGHT AN END TO IT YOUR-SELF.
I'M SURE YOU WOULD'VE WANTED ZERO TO BE HERE WITH YOU AS WELL.

LONG TIME NO SEE.
UH-HUH.
AI MADE IT THROUGH.
HOW ARE YOU?
THEY'VE BEEN WORKING ME HARD.
SHFF

—7—

(continued ↓)

And so, the special series *Memories* is filled with the selfishness of its creator.

If I am asked why I keep working on it, the immediate answer that comes to mind is "as long as there are people who want to read my work, I want to enjoy this series with those readers." I'll keep doing my best.

Please enjoy volume 3, which is scheduled to come out next year!

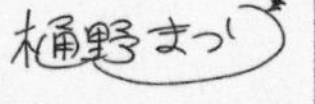

Matsuri Hino

YUKI AND I MEET HERE AT THE EDGE OF THE CROSS ACADEMY CAMPUS. A FEW YEARS HAVE PASSED SINCE WE DECIDED THAT.
THE PEOPLE WHO DO NOT SUPPORT OUR RELATIONSHIP AREN'T ABLE TO SPY ON US HERE.
THOUGH IT'S NOT LIKE OUR RELATIONSHIP WOULD MAKE DRASTIC PROGRESS HERE ANYWAY...
I FOUND MYSELF...
...BEING TOPPLED BY HER.
AI'S GRACIOUS-NESS AND NOBLE-NESS...
...ARE SO STRIKING.
I THOUGHT, "COMPARED TO HER, I'M..."
BUT AT THE SAME TIME, I FELT RELIEVED.
I'VE MADE IT THIS FAR, AND I DIDN'T FAIL.

I DIDN'T HARM THE TREASURE...
...THAT MAN LEFT IN MY CARE.
HM...?
OH NO, WHY...
I GUESS I WAS OVER-COME BY EMOTION.

YOU'VE DONE WELL...
I KNOW WHO THOSE TEARS ARE FOR.
BUT...
...SHE DOESN'T SHOW HER WEAKNESSES TO ANYONE BUT ME.

THAT NOTICE ...
"TO PROTECT THE SAFETY OF OUR CUSTOMERS, WE WILL NOT BE DOING BUSINESS AFTER SUNSET FOR THE TIME BEING."
SOMEONE TRIED TO KIDNAP A CHILD FROM THE SHOP, AND THE KIDNAPPER ESCAPED.
DO THEY THINK A VAMPIRE IS AT FAULT?
THERE ISN'T A LOT OF PROOF, BUT THEY ASSUME SO.
DON'T WORRY ABOUT IT.
IT'S ONLY NATURAL FOR HUMANS TO BE CAUTIOUS OF UNKNOWN CREATURES.
SOME HAVE EXPRESSED POSITIVE VIEWS ABOUT US TOO.

I DON'T KNOW IF THIS IS THANKS TO THE SEEDS PLANTED BY PRESIDENT CROSS AT HIS ACADEMY...
...BUT THE CURRENT SITUATION IS PROBABLY A MILLION TIMES BETTER THAN THOSE CONFLICTS IN THE PAST.
THERE WAS A TIME WHEN HUMANS ERASED THE VERY EXISTENCE OF VAMPIRES FROM THEIR HISTORY JUST TO LIVE PEACEFULLY...
WHAT DO YOU THINK, HANABUSA? DOESN'T THEIR PREJUDICE HURT YOUR FEELINGS?
WHAT I THINK HARDLY MATTERS!
?
BECAUSE!
I HAVE A WONDERFUL WOMAN WHO CARES FOR ME DEEPLY.
AND THAT WOMAN IS HUMAN.
AAH.
THE STARS ARE SO BEAUTIFUL TONIGHT!

I'M MEMORIZING EVERY MOMENT...
...OF LOOKING UP AT THIS BEAUTIFUL STARRY SKY WITH YOU.
AS LONG AS I LIVE...
...THIS MEMORY WILL REMAIN.
I CAN'T SEE ANY STARS...
THEY'RE THERE!
SO BEAUTI-FUL.

A LITTLE WHILE AFTER THAT, AT THE USUAL BENCH...
...YUKI SAID SOME-THING LIKE THIS...
NO MATTER HOW DIFFICULT THE PATH MAY BE, THEY CAN OVERCOME IT AS LONG AS THEY'RE TOGETHER.
MARRIED COUPLES LIKE THAT ARE NICE, AREN'T THEY?
SHE SEEMED TO BE PONDERING SOME-THING...
...AND TRYING TO COME TO A DECISION.
I SIMPLY WATCHED HER.
OUR RELATIONSHIP HASN'T CHANGED AT ALL.
STILL...

Acknowledgements

I would like to thank my editor, the graphic novel editor, the designer, the printer and everyone else involved in making this volume.

To the people who lend me their full support to complete my final drafts:
O. Mio-sama
K. Midori-sama
A. Ichiya-sama

To my family and friends who support me behind the scenes.

And most of all, to the readers.

Thank you very much.

-Hino

Thank you very much for your letters too! I read through every one of them!!

A COUNCIL WAS ESTABLISHED TO SOLVE...

...PROBLEMS UNIQUE TO US THAT CANNOT BE DEALT WITH BY HUMAN SOCIETY.

AND THEN THERE WERE PRESIDENT CROSS'S STRANGE SEMINARS...
"SHIKI AND RIMA HAVE NOT AGED AT ALL! ARE THEY VAMPIRES?!"
"THERE MUST BE OTHERS WHO WORK IN SOCIETY WITHOUT REVEALING THEIR IDENTITIES! WHAT ARE THEY UP TO?!"
PLUB
Weekly GOSSIP
THAT'S WRITTEN RIGHT HERE IN THIS TABLOID!
EVEN PURE-HEARTED TAX-PAYING CITIZENS LIKE THEM AREN'T EXEMPT FROM THIS!!

THAT'S WHY I MADE A GRAPH OF THE PAST TEN YEARS TO COMPARE THE CRIME RATE...

...BY DEGREE OF VIOLENCE BETWEEN HUMANS AND VAMP— I MEAN, NOCTURNAL PEOPLE WITH A BLOOD-LOVING PROCLIVITY, AS THEY'RE CALLED TODAY!

LOOK! ISN'T IT CLEAR?

YES, THAT'S ASTOUNDING! THERE'S HARDLY ANY DIFFERENCE!

I WANT TO CLEAR UP THE MISUNDER-STANDINGS...

...BUT JUST GRAPHS WON'T DO.

WE NEED TO HEAR FROM THE PEOPLE.

THAT IS WHY I HAVE A FAVOR TO ASK YOU, KAGEYAMA, BECAUSE YOU'RE A GOVERNMENT OFFICIAL...

...AND YOU, SAYORI, BECAUSE YOU HAVE EXPERIENCE BEING A POLITICIAN'S ASSISTANT.

WILL YOU HELP?

I WANT YOU TO SPEAK TO PARLIA-MENT—

I'LL DO IT! I'LL DO IT FOR RUKA!

I'M...
...AGAINST IT.
SUFF SUFF
WHY...?
IF YOU REENTER SOCIETY, YOU MAY END UP BEING TARGETED BY DUBIOUS STRANGERS AGAIN.
BUT NOTHING HAS HAP-PENED SINCE THEN.
WON'T IT BE BETTER TO SPEAK OUT IN PUBLIC SO PEOPLE WILL NOTICE?
IT WOULD BE DIFFICULT FOR THEM TO ATTACK A PERSON WHO IS SPEAKING IN PARLIA-MENT.
HM?
MRRR
HMM...

YOU'VE BEEN KEPT SAFE BECAUSE I MADE AN EFFORT TO PROTECT YOU MYSELF.
AND I VOW TO CONTINUE TO PROTECT YOU.
BUT IF YOU DO THIS, I NEED YOUR PROMISE THAT YOU WILL NOT DIE SO EASILY.
WOULD IT BE ALL RIGHT IF I ASKED YUKI...
...TO TURN YOU INTO ONE OF US?
SLAP

I WAS PROUD...
...THAT YOU LOVED ME AS A HUMAN BEING.
YET I'VE ALWAYS FELT INDEBTED TO YOU FOR THAT.
I'M SO SORRY.
I'VE BEEN WRONG ALL THIS TIME...
I'M SORRY...
DASH

CHAK
VROOOM
IT'S OKAY— YOU'RE COMING TOO!
SAYORI...?
WAAAAAH
DASH

SAYORI!!
LISTEN TO ME, YUKI...
I KNEW I'D DIE A LOT EARLIER THAN HANABUSA, BUT I THOUGHT THERE MUST BE A GOOD REASON FOR THAT.
SO I PLANNED TO MAKE THE MOST OF MY LIFE.
I HAVE A MISSION TO CARRY OUT.
BUT...
...I WAS ONLY GETTING CARRIED AWAY.

I MIGHT AS WELL...
HOW CAN I CONTINUE DOING SOME-THING THAT HANABUSA CAN'T SUPPORT...
...WITH HIS WHOLE HEART?
SAYORI!!
STAY BACK!
JUST LIKE HOW THERE ARE THINGS THAT ONLY HANABUSA CAN DO BECAUSE OF ALL THE TIME HE HAS...
...THERE IS SOMETHING ONLY I CAN DO BECAUSE I'M THE HUMAN HANABUSA LOVES.
AFTER GIVING BIRTH TO MY CHILD, I FINALLY WAS ABLE TO FIGURE OUT WHAT THAT WAS.

I WANT TO LEAVE A WORLD IN WHICH THE ONE I LOVE AND OUR CHILD CAN LIVE WITH THEIR HEADS HELD HIGH...
...FOR WHO THEY ARE.
RIGHT.
EVERYONE HAS THE GRANDEST DREAMS FOR THEIR CHILD...
I'M ACTUALLY ALL FOR THAT!!!
BUT... DON'T YOU SEE?
IT'S NOT WRONG OF ME TO WISH FOR THE PERSON I LOVE TO LIVE A LONG AND PEACEFUL LIFE.

I STILL...
...WANT TO SEE YOU SHINE AS BRIGHTLY AS YOU CAN.
I WANT TO BRAG TO OUR CHILD ABOUT YOU.
I WASN'T READY TO FACE YOUR MORTALI-TY...
...BUT I'LL PREPARE MYSELF.
I WILL NOT TRAMPLE OVER THE DECISION YOU MADE!
WAAH...
AH...
THERE, THERE...
WAAH.
I'M SORRY. I'M SORRY...

KYAH
MAA!
KYAH
NOW, NOW.
THAT'S A GOOD CHILD.
YOU'VE GROWN SO BIG!
YOU'RE SO CUTE AND CHUBBY.♡
SMITTEN
...
LET'S GO HOME.
WHAT?!
HUH?
BUT NOTHING HAS BEEN SOLVED.
ONE THING HAS.
I'VE REALIZED I MUST SPEND MY WHOLE LIFE PROVING TO YOU THAT THE HUMAN ME...
...IS NOT THAT WEAK.

I'LL KEEP WORKING HARD AT THAT...
...SO IT'S STILL OKAY TO LET YOU PAMPER ME SO MUCH, RIGHT?

HEY.
YUKI.
HM?
CAN'T WE...
...BE LIKE THAT TOO?
WHY DON'T WE...
...HOLD HANDS FOR A CHANGE?

WHY IS IT THAT...

...I CAN'T HELP REMEMBERING HIM WHEN I DO THIS.
ME TOO.
BUT...
...THAT'S NOT A PROBLEM.
KLASP

YUKI...
I LOVE YOU IN YOUR ENTIRETY WITH HIM INSIDE YOU.
GRIP
SHK
...

...
I DON'T RESPOND TO YOUR FEELINGS, AND I DON'T LET YOU GO.
SO WHY DO YOU...
YOU HAVE KIND HANDS.
THESE HANDS SAVED ME NUMEROUS TIMES.
WHEN I SEE YOU SMILING...
PRUMP
...IT MAKES ME HAPPY.

IT HAS TO BE YOU.
SHE DIDN'T ANSWER ME.
BUT A LITTLE WHILE LATER...
...YUKI TOOK THE INITIATIVE...
...AND HELD MY HAND.
I...
...TAKE THAT AS A POSITIVE SIGN.

I WAIT FOR MY CHANCE...

...WHILE INDULGING IN OUR LAZY, COMFORTING AND UNPRODUCTIVE RELATIONSHIP.
WE GET SCOLDED AT TIMES.

WE CHEER EACH OTHER UP...
...LICK EACH OTHER'S WOUNDS...

...AND WE MOURNED THE DEATH OF OUR FRIENDS TOGETHER SEVERAL TIMES.

ON THE WAY BACK FROM THE FUNERALS...
...IT WAS ALWAYS MY JOB TO SOOTHE YUKI'S FEELINGS.
WE WERE LEFT BEHIND...
...BY OUR CHANGING SURROUNDINGS.
AND...
SAYORI, I UNDERSTAND.
I HAVE TO FOLLOW IN YOUR FOOTSTEPS.
I PROMISE.
YOU WERE MY STAR ON EARTH.

THEN, AFTER HALF THE SEASONS PASSED...

...AND BEFORE WE KNEW IT, ALL THOSE WHO WERE AGAINST OUR RELATIONSHIP WERE GONE.

I KNOW IT'S IMPOSSIBLE...

...BUT THIS FEELING WON'T DISAPPEAR.

IT HAPPENED ONE DAY WHEN I WAS OFF WORK.

I WANT TO BRING HIM BACK TO LIFE. I WANT HIM TO DEVOUR MY LIFE, AND I WANT TO RETURN INSIDE HIM.
I MUST BE CRAZY BECAUSE THAT WILL NEVER HAPPEN.
BUT THIS FEELING WON'T GO AWAY...
I THOUGHT I'D HAVE TO MOVE FORWARD...
...INTO THIS FUTURE ALONE WITH THIS LINGERING EMOTION.
BUT...
...I HAD AI...
...AND YOU WERE ALWAYS BESIDE ME.

BECAUSE OF YOU...
...I'M STILL ABLE TO SMILE LIKE THIS.

ZERO KIRYU.
I'M A PUREBLOOD VAMPIRE...
...BUT WOULD YOU BE WILLING TO START A RELATIONSHIP WITH ME?
HEH
WHAT WAS THAT...
AND THAT'S HOW...
...WE STARTED AGAIN.

IT MAKES ME HAPPY TO SEE YOU SMILE TOO, ZERO.
I'M SO GLAD...

YOU ARE MY NORTH STAR/END

EDITOR'S NOTES

CHARACTERS

Matsuri Hino puts careful thought into the names of her characters in *Vampire Knight*. Below is the collection of characters throughout the manga. Each character's name is presented family name first, per the kanji reading.

黒主優姫

Cross Yuki

Yuki's last name, *Kurosu*, is the Japanese pronunciation of the English word "cross." However, the kanji has a different meaning—*kuro* means "black" and *su* means "master." Her first name is a combination of *yuu*, meaning "tender" or "kind," and *ki*, meaning "princess."

錐生零

Kiryu Zero

Zero's first name is the kanji for *rei*, meaning "zero." In his last name, *Kiryu*, the *ki* means "auger" or "drill" and the *ryu* means "life."

玖蘭枢

Kuran Kaname

Kaname means "hinge" or "door." The kanji for his last name is a combination of the old-fashioned way of writing *ku*, meaning "nine," and *ran*, meaning "orchid": "nine orchids."

藍堂英

Aido Hanabusa

Hanabusa means "petals of a flower." *Aido* means "indigo temple." In Japanese, the pronunciation of *Aido* is very close to the pronunciation of the English word *idol*.

架院暁

Kain Akatsuki

Akatsuki means "dawn" or "daybreak." In *Kain, ka* is a base or support, while *in* denotes a building that has high fences around it, such as a temple or school.

早園瑠佳

Souen Ruka

In *Ruka*, the *ru* means "lapis lazuli" while the *ka* means "good-looking" or "beautiful." The *sou* in Ruka's surname, *Souen*, means "early," but this kanji also has an obscure meaning of "strong fragrance." The *en* means "garden."

一条拓麻

Ichijo Takuma

Ichijo can mean a "ray" or "streak." The kanji for *Takuma* is a combination of *taku*, meaning "to cultivate," and *ma*, which is the kanji for *asa*, meaning "hemp" or "flax," a plant with blue flowers.

支葵千里

Shiki Senri

Shiki's last name is a combination of *shi*, meaning "to support" and *ki*, meaning "mallow"—a flowering plant with pink or white blossoms. The *ri* in *Senri* is a traditional Japanese unit of measure for distance, and one *ri* is about 2.44 miles. *Senri* means "1,000 *ri*."

夜刈十牙

Yagari Toga

Yagari is a combination of *ya*, meaning "night," and *gari*, meaning "to harvest." *Toga* means "ten fangs."

一条麻遠, 一翁

Ichijo Asato, a.k.a. "Ichio"

Ichijo can mean a "ray" or "streak." Asato's first name is comprised of *asa*, meaning "hemp" or "flax," and *tou*, meaning "far-off." His nickname is *ichi*, or "one," combined with *ou*, which can be used as an honorific when referring to an older man.

若葉沙頼

Wakaba Sayori

Yori's full name is Sayori Wakaba. *Wakaba* means "young leaves." Her given name, *Sayori*, is a combination of *sa*, meaning "sand," and *yori*, meaning "trust."

星煉

Seiren

Sei means "star" and *ren* means "to smelt" or "to refine." *Ren* is also the same kanji used in *rengoku*, or "purgatory." Her previous name, *Hoshino*, uses the same kanji for "star" (*hoshi*) and *no*, which can mean "from" and is often used at the end of traditional female names.

遠矢莉磨

Toya Rima

Toya means a "far-reaching arrow." Rima's first name is a combination of *ri*, or "jasmine," and *ma*, which signifies enhancement by wearing away, such as by polishing or scouring.

紅まり亜

Kurenai Maria

Kurenai means "crimson." The kanji for the last *a* in Maria's first name is the same that is used in "Asia."

錐生壱縷

Kiryu Ichiru

Ichi is the old-fashioned way of writing "one" and *ru* means "thread." In *Kiryu*, the *ki* means "auger" or "drill" and the *ryu* means "life."

緋桜閑, 狂咲姫

Hio Shizuka, Kuruizaki-hime

Shizuka means "calm and quiet." In Shizuka's family name, *hi* is "scarlet" and *ou* is "cherry blossoms." Shizuka Hio is also referred to as the "Kuruizaki-hime." *Kuruizaki* means "flowers blooming out of season" and *hime* means "princess."

藍堂月子

Aido Tsukiko

Aido means "indigo.temple." *Tsukiko* means "moon child."

白蕗更

Shirabuki Sara

Shira is "white" and *buki* is "butterbur," a plant with white flowers. *Sara* means "to renew."

黒主灰閻

Cross Kaien

Cross, or *Kurosu*, means "black master." *Kaien* is a combination of *kai*, meaning "ashes," and *en*, meaning "village gate." The kanji for *en* is also used for Enma, the ruler of the underworld in Buddhist mythology.

玖蘭李土

Kuran Rido

Kuran means "nine orchids." In *Rido*, *ri* means "plum" and *do* means "earth."

玖蘭樹里

Kuran Juri

Kuran means "nine orchids." In her first name, *ju* means "tree" and a *ri* is a traditional Japanese unit of measure for distance. The kanji for *ri* is the same as in Senri's name.

玖蘭悠

Kuran Haruka

Kuran means "nine orchids." *Haruka* means "distant" or "remote."

鷹宮海斗

Takamiya Kaito

Taka means "hawk" and *miya* means "imperial palace" or "shrine." *Kai* is "sea" and *to* means "to measure" or "grid."

菖藤依砂也

Shoto Isaya

Sho means "Siberian iris" and *to* is "wisteria." The *I* in *Isaya* means "to rely on" while the *sa* means "sand." *Ya* is a suffix used for emphasis.

橙茉

Toma

In the family name *Toma, to* means "Seville orange" and *ma* means "jasmine flower."

藍堂永路

Aido Nagamichi

The name *Nagamichi* is a combination of *naga*, which means "long" or "eternal," and *michi*, which is the kanji for "road" or "path." *Aido* means "indigo temple."

縹木

Hanadagi

In this family name, *hanada* means "bright light blue" and *gi* means "tree."

影山霞

Kageyama Kasumi

In the Class Rep's family name, *kage* means "shadow" and *yama* means "mountain." His first name, *Kasumi*, means "haze" or "mist."

愛

Ai

Ai means "love." It is used in terms of unconditional, unending love and affection.

Ren

Ren means "love." It is used in terms of a romantic love or crush.

Terms

-sama: The suffix *-sama* is used in formal address for someone who ranks higher in the social hierarchy. The vampires call their leader "Kaname-sama" only when they are among their own kind.

Renai: The combination of Ren's and Ai's names (恋愛) means "romantic love."

Matsuri Hino burst onto the manga scene with her title *Kono Yume ga Sametara* (When This Dream Is Over), which was published in *LaLa DX* magazine. Hino was a manga artist a mere nine months after she decided to become one.

With the success of her popular series *Captive Hearts*, *MeruPuri* and *Vampire Knight*, Hino is a major player in the world of shojo manga.

Hino enjoys creative activities and has commented that she would have been either an architect or an apprentice to traditional Japanese craftsmasters if she had not become a manga artist.

VAMPIRE KNIGHT: MEMORIES
Vol. 2
Shojo Beat Manga Edition

STORY AND ART BY
MATSURI HINO

Adaptation/Nancy Thistlethwaite
Translation/Tetsuichiro Miyaki
Touch-Up Art & Lettering/Inori Fukuda Trant
Graphic Design/Alice Lewis
Editor/Nancy Thistlethwaite

Printed in the U.S.A.

Published by VIZ Media, LLC
P.O. Box 77010
San Francisco, CA 94107

10 9 8 7 6 5 4 3 2 1
First printing, August 2018

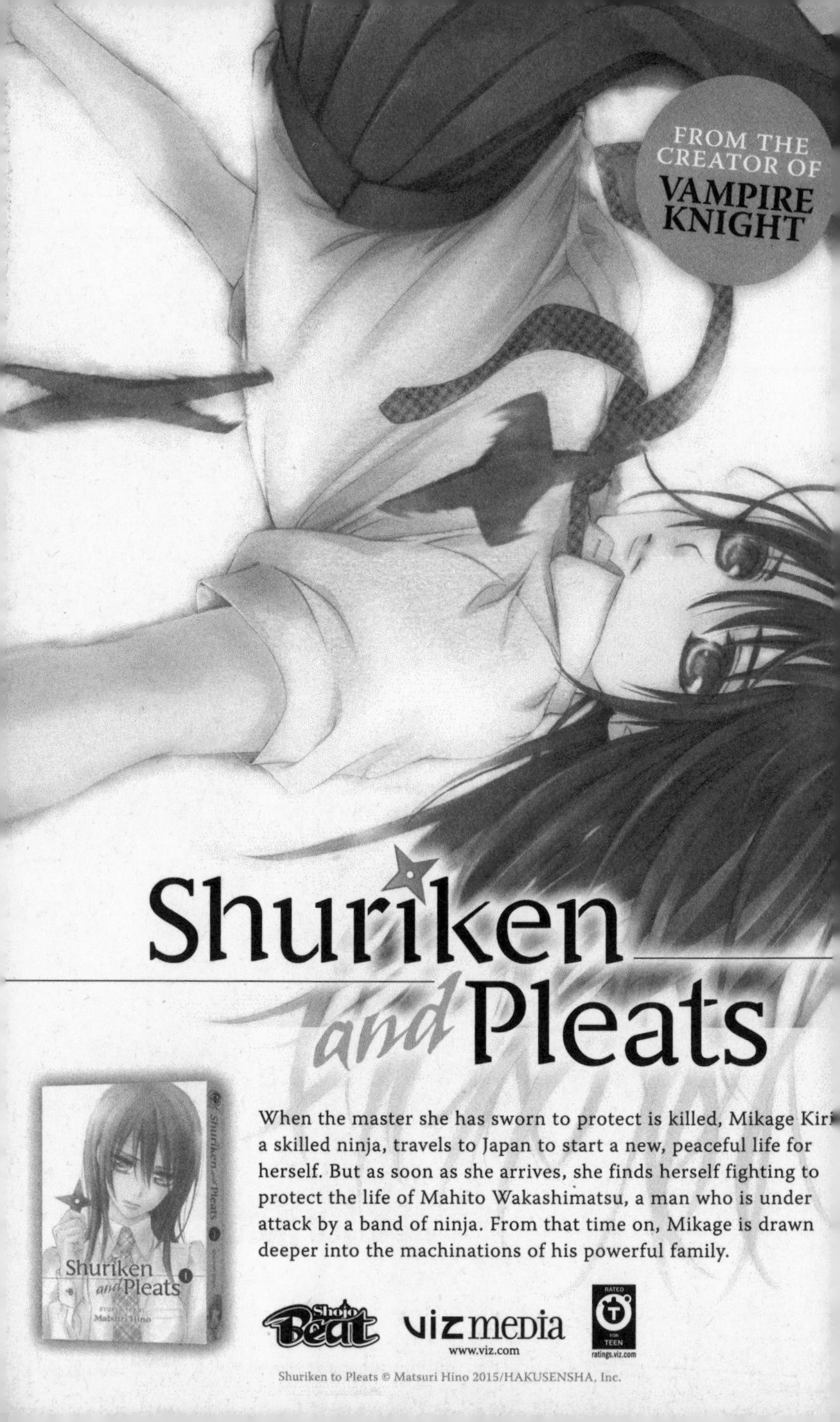